Nature

Describing a picture

1 Look. What can you see? Write (✔) or (✗).

1 three rocks ✗

2 three trees ☐

3 five flowers ☐

4 the sun ☐

5 two clouds ☐

6 six spiders ☐

2 Now read and check.

In the picture, there are four flowers. Next to the flowers there are two rocks. There are six ants on the rocks. Next to the rocks there are three trees. Behind the rocks there is a pond. The sun is in the sky. Next to the sun there are two big clouds. It is sunny and cloudy. Under the clouds there are five birds.

3 Read again. Then circle.

1 The (rocks)/ *birds* are next to the flowers.

2 There are *four* / *five* birds.

3 The birds are *under* / *next to* the clouds.

4 There is a pond *behind* / *next to* the rocks.

5 It is *windy* / *cloudy*.

T0352396

④ Match the two parts of the words.

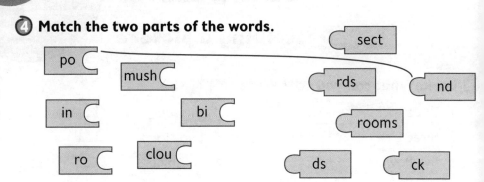

po | sect

mush | rds

nd

in | bi

rooms

ro | clou | ds | ck

⑤ Find four insects.

shantsrewormsnibutterfliesepspidersdo

⑥ Read and complete.

There are six spiders plus thirteen ants in the garden. That equals ¹ _____ insects.

There are twelve books on nature in the library plus eight dictionaries. That equals ² _____ books.

There are twenty children in the playground plus thirty in the classroom. That equals ³ _____ children in the school.

⑦ Write. Then match.

1 14 + 5 = _Fourteen plus five equals_ _____   a eighteen

2 30 + 10 = _____   b nineteen

3 6 + 12 = _____   c ten

4 17 + 13 = _____   d forty

5 2 + 8 =   _____   e thirty

Remember

There **is** one flower	There **are** two flowers
There **is** one ant	There **are** six ants

8 **Draw a nature picture. Then write.**

- What's in the picture?
- How many birds, ants and trees are there?
- Where are they?

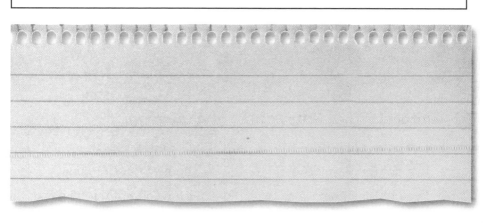

2 Me

Writing a description

1 Read. Then draw.

I'm Rita. I'm a woman. I've got a small nose and a big mouth. I've got long eyelashes. I've got short red hair and green eyes. I've got brown glasses. I've got a round chin and a short neck.

I'm Andrew. I'm a man. I've got a big nose and a small mouth. I've got thick eyebrows and thick eyelashes. I've got long grey hair and brown eyes. I've got a grey moustache. I've got a long neck.

2 Read again. Then write R (Rita) or A (Andrew).

1 I've got a big nose. **A**

2 I've got long eyelashes. ☐

3 I've got long hair. ☐

4 I've got glasses. ☐

5 I haven't got red hair. ☐

6 I haven't got a long neck. ☐

3 **Match. Then draw.**

1	blond	**a**	eyes
2	thick	**b**	eyebrows
3	blue	**c**	hair
4	long	**d**	hair

4 **Read. Then circle.**

1 broad *fingernails /* (*shoulders*)

2 long *eyelashes / chin*

3 a flat *arm / stomach*

4 strong *eyes / arms*

5 short *fingernails / stomach*

6 a round *eyelash / chin*

5 **Look and write. Use the words from the box.**

a man	men	a woman	women	people

1 _a woman_

2 _____

3 _____

4 _____

5 _____

2 Describing someone

6 **Draw a picture of a man or a woman. Then describe him / her. Use words from the unit.**

Has he / she got blond / brown hair?

Has he / she got broad shoulders?

Has he / she got a round chin?

Pets  3

Giving instructions

1 Read. What is Bip?

Bip is a _____ .

Hi, Jenny!
Thank you so much for looking after Bip in August!
He's very good. Here are the instructions for him:
At 8 o'clock, take him out for a walk.
When you get back, please wash his paws if they are dirty.
At 9 o'clock, give him some dog biscuits for breakfast.
Put more water in his water bowl.
Then put him in the garden.
At 6 o'clock, give him some meat and some dog biscuits.
Take him out for a short walk at 8.30.
He goes to bed at 9 o'clock. Please put him in his bed.
Thank you!
Gemma xx

2 Read again. Then number the instructions in order.

☐ Put more water in his water bowl.

☐ Please put him in his bed.

☐ When you get back, please wash his paws if they are dirty.

☐ Then put him in the garden.

3 Animal body parts

3 Look and write.

| tail | beak | wings | paws | whiskers | feathers | claws | fur |

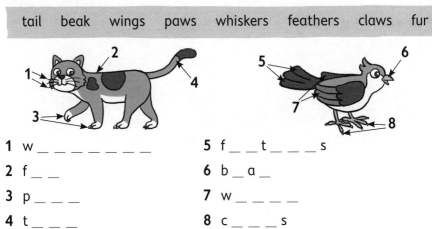

1 w _ _ _ _ _ _ _ _   5 f _ _ t _ _ _ s
2 f _ _   6 b _ a _
3 p _ _ _   7 w _ _ _ _
4 t _ _ _   8 c _ _ _ s

4 Match the opposites.

1 soft   **a** slow

2 smooth   **b** scary

3 cute   **c** hard

4 fast   **d** sharp

5 Unscramble. Then write.

Lifecycle of the butterfly

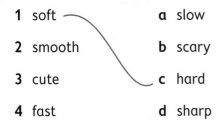

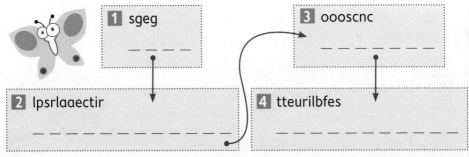

1 sgeg

_ _ _ _ _

2 lpsrlaaectir

_ _ _ _ _ _ _ _ _ _ _

3 oooscnc

_ _ _ _ _ _ _

4 tteurilbfes

_ _ _ _ _ _ _ _ _ _ _

Remember!

We usually write instructions in order.

At 9 o'clock, take him out for a walk.

Then put him in the garden.

In the afternoon, take him for a walk.

⑥ Your friend is looking after your pet. Write instructions.

- What is your pet's name?
- What time does he / she eat? What does he / she eat?
- What does he / she drink? How much?
- Where and when does he / she go to sleep?
- What else does your friend need to do?

Dear _____,

Thank you for looking after _____

_____

_____

_____

_____

_____

_____

_____

_____

4 Home

Describing a house

1 **Read. Then circle.**

House for sale!
This house is in a village, opposite the church. It's got four bedrooms. All the bedrooms have got wardrobes. There are mirrors in the bedrooms. There are two bathrooms. The bathrooms have got a mirror and a shower. Outside, there is a garage for two cars and a big garden.

Flat for sale!
This flat is in the centre of the town. It's next to the park. It's got two bedrooms and a bathroom. It hasn't got a garden but it's got a big balcony. There is a garage in the basement of the building.

1 The house is *next to* / *opposite* the church.

2 The house *has got* / *hasn't got* a balcony.

3 In the house, there are wardrobes in the *two* / *four* bedrooms.

4 The flat is *next to* / *opposite* the park.

5 The flat *has* / *hasn't* got a basement.

2 **Read again. Then write (✔).**

	House	Flat
1 It's got four wardrobes.	✔	☐
2 There's one bathroom.	☐	☐
3 It has got a balcony.	☐	☐
4 It's next to the park.	☐	☐
5 There is a big garden.	☐	☐
6 It's got two bedrooms.	☐	☐

3 Read. Then draw.

There's a bin under the table. There's a cat behind the chair. There is a cupboard next to the table. Next to the wardrobe, on the right, there is a tall plant. There is a small plant below the window. There is a dog in front of the table.

4 Read. Then find and write.

1 You clean your teeth with this. _____toothbrush_____

2 You wash your hair with this. _____

3 This keeps you warm in bed. _____

4 You put your clothes in this. _____

5 You put your car in this. _____

6 This is a place to sit outside. _____

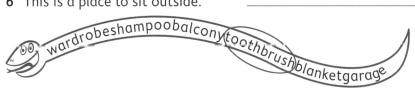

wardrobeshampoobalconytoothbrushblanketgarage

4 Describing a house

5 **Write about a house or flat.**

- Where is it? What is next to / opposite it?
- How many bedrooms has it got? What is in them?
- Has it got a garden or balcony? Where is it? What's in / on it?
- Is there a garage?

Clothes

A list

1 Read the list. Write (✔) what you need for a sleepover.

toothbrush		trainers	
shorts		T-shirt	
butterfly		sofa	
comb		jeans	
rock		belt	

2 Read. Then draw what's missing.

woolly jumper

hiking boots

colourful ski jacket

blue jeans

plain scarf

socks

blue cotton T-shirt

leather belt

hat

3 Match. Then write.

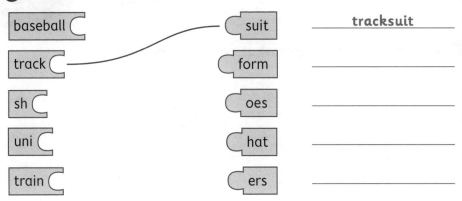

baseball	suit
track	form
sh	oes
uni	hat
train	ers

tracksuit

_____

_____

_____

_____

4 Draw and colour. Then write. Use the words from the box.

beanie   boots   brown   colourful   fancy   jumper   leather
orange   plain   red   scarf   dress   tights   woolly

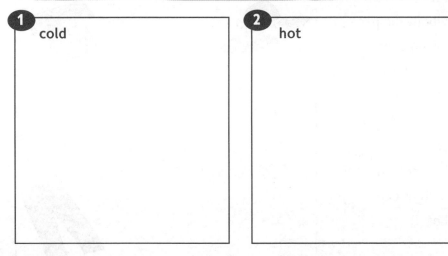

1 cold

2 hot

It's cold. I'm wearing

_____

_____ .

It's hot. I'm wearing

_____

_____ .

Remember!

a green T-shirt, a purple scarf, an orange hat

black trousers, pink pyjamas

5 Read. Then correct.

1 I've got trousers grey.

   I've got grey trousers.

2 I've got a hat woolly.

_____

3 I've got a white socks.

_____

4 I've got T-shirt cotton.

_____

6 Write a list for a sleepover. Then draw.

6 Sports

A news bulletin

1 **Read the news bulletin. Circle four more mistakes.**

Parkhill School sports day

When	What	Who	Where
09.00	volleyball	Reds v Yellows	on the beach
10.00	basketball	Blues v Yellows	basketball court in the gym
11.30	tennis	Greens v Reds	tennis court
12.15	running (100 metres)	All	track in stadium

End of year sports day news

It's the last week and it's sports day. The day starts with volleyball. Reds are playing Yellows in the gym at 9.00. The basketball game is in the stadium at 10.00. Blues and Yellows are playing. The third sport is tennis. That's on the basketball court at 11.30. Greens are playing Reds. The fourth sport is the 100 metres. That's on the beach at 12.15. Everyone is running.

2 **Read again. Then correct.**

1 The volleyball game is on the beach.

2 _____

3 _____

4 _____

5 _____

3 Write.

> climb   play   ride   do   catch

_____ _____ _____ _____ _____

4 Read. Then match the pairs.

1 basketball   **a** pool
2 bowling   **b** court
3 swimming   **c** track
4 skating   **d** alley
5 running   **e** rink
6 ski   **f** slope

5 Unscramble. Then write.

> runt   tcserth   stiwt   dnbe

1 <u>S t r e t c h</u> your arms.
2 _ _ _ _ your knees.
3 _ _ _ _ _ _ your body to the left.
4 _ _ _ _ around.

6 A news bulletin

6 Read. Then write. Use the words from the box.

basketball   football   karate   running   skating   skiing
swimming   taekwondo   tennis   volleyball

I love playing ...   I love going ...   I love doing ...

basketball   _____   _____

_____   _____   _____

_____   _____   _____

_____   _____   _____

7 Write the programme for a sports day. Then write a news bulletin.

Sports day programme

What   Where

_____   _____

_____   _____

_____   _____

SPORTS DAY NEWS

_____

_____

_____

Food 7

A menu

1 **What's your favourite food? Write.**

_____

_____

2 **Look at the menu. Then circle.**

Today's menu

Salads

Potato and tomato salad	☺	☹
Green salad	☹	☹
Avocado and lettuce salad	☺	☺

Pizzas

Cheese and tomato	☺	☺
Broccoli, spinach and egg	☺	☹
Cheese and mushroom	☹	☺

Desserts

Strawberries and ice cream	☺	☺
Fruit salad with mango, papaya, peaches and cherries	☹	☺

1 Does he like green salad?   Yes / No

2 Do they like cheese and tomato pizza?   Yes / No

3 Do they like avocado and lettuce salad?   Yes / No

4 Does she like strawberries and ice cream?   Yes / No

5 Does she like cheese and mushroom pizza?   Yes / No

7 Food plurals

3 Write the plural.

1 potato   <u>potatoes</u>   4 cherry _____

2 carrot _____   5 orange _____

3 avocado _____   6 mango _____

4 Read and sort. Then write. Use the words from the box.

| apricots | cabbage | carrots | cucumber | lettuce | papaya |
| peaches | spinach | strawberries | watermelon |

Fruit	Vegetables
apricots	

5 Look. Find these words.

~~dairy~~

fats

grains

healthy

protein

sugars

unhealthy

H	G	R	A	I	N	S	T	Y	O	S	D
P	H	L	R	Y	U	U	D	C	B	I	K
R	E	A	Y	J	K	G	U	F	A	T	S
B	A	O	P	C	D	A	B	H	K	I	W
S	L	D	H	G	P	R	O	T	E	I	N
L	T	E	L	F	E	S	A	J	K	E	O
G	H	C	I	D	A	I	R	Y	L	C	P
S	Y	B	S	T	W	U	E	T	R	A	U
H	U	N	H	E	A	L	T	H	Y	O	F
D	O	E	S	A	D	F	W	R	C	P	O

Remember!

Plural of words ending in -y:

cherry ⇨ cherries   strawberry ⇨ strawberries

6 **Write a menu for a party. Use words from the unit. Think:**

- When is the party?
- What are you celebrating?
- Is there any special food?
- What foods do your friends like?
- What don't they like?

Party menu

_____

_____

_____

_____

_____

_____

_____

_____

_____

_____

_____

_____

A dialogue

1 **Read. What instrument is Ann playing?**

Ann is playing the _____ .

Mum:	Is that you, Ann?
Ann:	Yes, Mum.
Mum:	What are you doing?
Ann:	I'm in the kitchen.
Mum:	You're making a lot of noise!
Ann:	Oh, sorry. I'm washing the dishes. There are no glasses!

(Ten minutes later ...)

Mum:	Where are you, Ann?
Ann:	I'm in my bedroom. I'm doing my homework.
Mum:	Mmm ... Are you playing the trumpet?
Ann:	Yes. And doing my homework. I've got music homework.
Mum:	Well, please play quietly.
Ann:	OK Mum.

2 **Read again. Then circle.**

1 In the kitchen, Ann is (washing the dishes) / drinking.

2 There are no clean *pots* / *glasses*.

3 In her bedroom, Ann is doing her *English* / *music* homework.

4 Ann is playing *quietly* / *loudly*.

5 Mum wants Ann to *play loudly* / *play quietly*.

Actions, adverbs of manner

3 Read and write ✔ = like or ✗ = don't like. Then add one more activity.

Things I like / don't like doing			
playing the piano		listening to music	
reading		eating	
dancing		cleaning the house	
singing		doing homework	
walking			

4 Look at Activity 3 and write.

I like _____ but I don't like _____ .

_____

_____

_____

_____

5 Read. Then write the opposite.

1 I don't like playing the piano quietly.

I like playing the piano _____ .

2 I don't like walking slowly. I _____

_____ .

6 Read. Then match.

1 set
2 tidy
3 make
4 do the
5 wash

a washing up
b the car
c the table
d my bed
e my bedroom

8 A dialogue

7 Read. Then write Susan, Jane or Mum.

Susan is doing her homework in the living room. Jane is sitting next to Susan. She's eating an apple. She's very noisy and Susan can't do her homework. Susan wants Jane to eat her apple quietly. But Jane is eating her apple loudly. Susan is angry. She wants Mum.

Where is Mum? Mum is in the kitchen. She's washing the dishes. Now Susan is in the kitchen, too. She's talking to Mum. Mum wants Jane to eat her apple in her bedroom!

Jane:	What are you doing?
	I'm doing my homework.
	What are you doing?
	I'm eating an apple.
	Jane is eating loudly. I can't do my homework.
	Jane, eat your apple in your bedroom, please!